The 20 Minute Film Pitch

A screenplay
By
Geoff Thompson

Geoff Thompson Limited
PO Box 307
Coventry
CV3 9YP
United Kingdom

www.geoffthompson.com

ISBN 9780956921581

Note:
This screenplay may not be performed without written permission from the publisher. Please write to the above address if you would like to discuss obtaining a licence to perform it.

DESIGN

Thank you to my gorgeous son Louis Thomson for our wonderful cover design.

SPECIAL THANKS

To **Warner Stephens**, my friend, thank you for financing this film, and for being so kind in your support of my work.

To **John Gore**, at the Warwick Arts Centre. Your support and friendship is very appreciated my friend.

To **Rory Nolan**, thank you for being so brave, for sharing your story with me, and allowing us the licence to weave it into a beautiful film.

To **'Hollywood' Steve Reynolds:** thank you for being so generous and sharing the director credit with me on this film, and also for guiding me through my first shot at film directing.

Thank you **Richard Adams** for bringing this film together so quickly, and so expertly and for so little money.

PRODUCTION TEAM

Starring – Rory Nolan
Director – Steve Reynolds
Director of Photography – Dave Cawley
Producers – Richard Adams and Warner Stephens
Gaffer – Seb Kudanowski
Sound – Billy Bannister
Script Supervisor – Daisy Spivey
Digital Transfer – David Tomlin
Colourist – Nat Higginbottom
Runner – Joe Sampson
Makeup & Hair – Hailey Walsh
Music – Phil Mountford
Writer/Director – Geoff Thompson

GEOFF THOMPSON

Geoff Thompson is a BAFTA winning Writer.

He has written over forty books (published in 21 languages), he is a multi-award-winning screenwriter, playwright (he was invited into the prestigious Royal Court Young Writers Group) and author of hundreds of articles, many published in national magazines and broadsheets, including *The Times*.

His stage play *Fragile* premiered to five star reviews at the Belgrade Theatre in 2012, and to critical acclaim at The Edinburgh Fringe Festival in 2014.

He also workshopped his most recent stage play, *Bindweed* at The national Theatre Studio in 2014.

CONTACT:
DAA Management
debi@daamanagement.co.uk
+44 (0) 207 255 6125

RORY NOLAN

Rory Nolan is an actor from Coventry.

He trained alongside the Royal Shakespeare Company at Stratford upon Avon College. After moving to London with Fluxx Theatre Company, Rory made his acting debut in the Sky TV sitcom *Trollied* opposite Jane Horrocks and Mark Addy. Rory also played 'Coop' in Shona Auerbach's film *Rudy*.

Geoff Thompson wrote **The 20 Minute Film Pitch** especially for Rory. The film is loosely based on Rory's life.

CONTACT:
rorynolan@ymail.com

STEPHEN REYNOLDS

From a background of self-funded short films, Writer/Director Stephen Reynolds blasted onto the UK film scene in 2013 with his debut feature *Vendetta* starring Danny Dyer, Vincent Regan (*300, Snow White and the Huntsman*) and Roxanne McKee (*Game of Thrones*).

He has since directed his first feature stateside for Lionsgate called *Lockdown* due for release in 2015.

CONTACT:
Via twitter
@reynoldsfilms

PRODUCERS

RICHARD ADAMS

Richard has been working on films since 2007, when he produced and financed *Within The Woods*, a zombie horror film. Since then he has produced and Line Produced three other features, including *The Somnambulists*, directed by Richard Jobson, which was shown at LIFF 2011.

More recently there has been a host of Shorts and Music promos, as well as time spent running both the Stratford Film Festival and The Convergence, a London based New Digital awareness seminar.

WARNER STEPHENS

Warner is an entrepreneur and Patron of the Arts, with a passion for British independent film.

This is the fourth collaboration with writer Geoff Thompson.

www.the20minutefilmpitch.com

INTRODUCTION

So…I'm on Skype talking to a deliciously eccentric young lad. I met him some time before, randomly in Coventry market. He was (he told me) an actor, and he'd recognised me from my books and films. We exchanged pleasantries. I liked him. He had something about him…*something*. I couldn't quantify what, but he was gentle, he was personable.

He certainly caught my attention.

After our initial encounter I never heard from him for about two years. Then one day out of the blue, my wife mentioned that a young actor had been in contact, looking for mentoring.

As well as writing films and plays and books, I also mentor people, and this lad wanted to book a session with me over Skype.

As soon as I saw his face on the computer screen I (of course) remembered him from our meeting in the market.

His name was Rory Nolan.

He said he wanted some advice on personal development and acting, *could I help*? I said I'd do my best but...we were only a few minutes into the conversation when I realised that Rory was not really looking for advice as much as he was (spontaneously) pitching me a film that he had been working on.

He wanted to know what I thought of his idea.

To be honest I can't even remember what his idea was, all I can recall is that I loved this kid; he was quirky, he was edgy, he was funny – a little scattered perhaps and definitely random, at times he was like a kite caught in the throes of a strong wind, *he was all over the place* (but in an exhilarating, inspired way). I had a real job keeping up with his machine-gun-chain-of-thought. But he was also profound – some of the things he said were *way* beyond his years – and more than anything else there was a purity about him. A purity that was unmistakable. An innocence that *could* be transcendent, if it was captured on screen.

I am not sure that anyone can quantify the Soul, but whatever it is, I experienced it through Rory on that Skype session. And I felt compelled (even commanded) to write down everything he was saying.

I asked him if he minded.

He was very happy for me to write as many notes as I wanted.

So I did.

As I wrote I asked him questions; about his film idea, about his acting, and latterly (more importantly) about his life.

His story was deeply moving. His story was beautifully tragic.

At times I think he actually forgot I was there.

He talked and I wrote and before we knew it an hour had passed and I had the beginnings of a story. Which is odd; he had not come to me asking for a film, and I definitely didn't receive him, looking for a script.

It just happened, an *accident*, one of those happy kinds that must be (in the words of Thomas Merton) "drawn up like a jewel from the bottom of the sea."

Afterwards I sat down for my tea – it was evening – but the idea (*and* the actor) would not leave me alone.

It wanted space on the page, *he* needed expression, and neither would wait, not even until the morning. The best stories are like that; they compel. These soulful diamonds are like *"divine creatures, shy and wild, secret and spontaneous"* (you don't find these kinds of scripts, *they* find you). They visit rarely, when *they* are ready, and when they do you have to capture them up immediately and home them on the page, lest they fly past and alight with some other scribe, one better attuned to his Pneuma, one more subservient to the command of intuition.

So I sat down with some urgency and let the story manifest through me.

In film terms (and in terms of the spirit – this is definitely from that place) you could say that this film *is* a happy accident. One of those blessings that you stumble upon when you are looking for something else.

I wrote it.

I presented it to Rory as a gift.

I thought it might work as a nice show-reel for him, some words he could throw at a camera and use to sell his wares as an actor.

But once it was on the page, it felt bigger than that.

Other people read the words and agreed; they loved it too.

My director friend, Steve Reynolds saw its merit and agreed to co-direct it with me as a film.

My friend Warner felt moved enough to fund the shoot.

Within about two months we had gone from conversation to celluloid.

We shot the film with a full crew over one day, and I have to tell you that Rory nailed it.

He was and he is absolute in this role.

I hope you enjoy reading the screenplay, and if you get a chance to watch the film proper, starring the *delightful bundle of quirk* that is Rory Nolan, I know you will love that too.

Geoff Thompson: December 2014

INT. HALLWAY – DAY

CLOSE ON *a door, in the hallway of a generic, anonymous hotel-like establishment.*
On the door is a sign: **Limbo Films – The 20 Minute Film Pitch.**
Sat outside is a nervous, quirky, 17 year old year old.
He is holding what looks like a film script.
We do not see the title of the film.
This is **GARY.**
A commanding voice from behind the closed door calls:

VOICE
Gary Smith?

Without obviously acknowledging the voice, Gary stands, turns and approaches the door.

CUT TO:

INT. HOTEL ROOM – CONTINUOUS

Inside the room we are on Gary, standing in front of a large boardroom table.
We are aware that there is someone behind the table, waiting for Gary's pitch, but he is in the shadows; we never actually see his face.
There is a **large hourglass sand-timer** *sat on the table.*

*The shadowy figure turns the timer over: the sand
start to fall through the neck of the hourglass.
The countdown begins.
Gary locks onto the timer with his eyes.
He watches the sand as it cascades.
Time is shifting quickly with each grain.
The timer appears to be the largest object in the room.
Gary has sweat on his brow.
He looks at the shadowy figure, sitting silently.*

GARY
I am pure love.

*Gary is waiting for a response.
There is no response.
Silence.
Gary tries again, more convincing this time.*

GARY (CONT'D)
I am...*pure* love.

*Gary looks at the figure behind the table.
Still nothing.
Gary looks at the timer.
(He does this periodically throughout the film).
He is patently aware that he is on the clock.*

GARY (CONT'D)
That's what the lead character says, right from the

off, **bang**, first line, before the titles, before the *you know*, before all the gubins, the shit, the fella in his swimming trunks hitting the big gong with his hammer, before the opening credits when you're fingering your popcorn, or texting your mate or titting up your girlfriend waiting for the action to start – *boom*. **I am pure love.**

(Beat)

That's his first line.
It's the opening line of the film...*and* at the end, at the very end of the film, final scene, the **cancer** scene the big cancer scene in the hospice where you're like fffffffffff...

(Blows emotionally through his lips)

...you get it; you know what I'm saying you **really** get it.
I am pure love!
Boom!
And that line makes no sense at all, not at the beginning of the film, which is what I want, it's intentional – I've set it up that way, start with confusion, *lead* the audience *you know*...the **wrong** way, set up the archetype, shatter the archetype when they least expect it – right through to revelation at the end when you're like whoaaaaaaaa, did not see

that coming, fucking hell, what is going on here, I thought this was a film about a warrior – 'cus the guy's like *built*, a fighter, some kind of divine angel or something but you're like *I get it now,* 'cus – I didn't tell you this, at the start of the film, at the very start of the film when he stands there, our lead man, staring straight into the screen like he's a stone cold dead-eyed warrior – and you don't know at this point that he's in a hospice, and that he's holding his mother in his arms and she is like all skin, she is all *damage* his mum, she is all skin and bone *a damaged shell* because the disease…the disease has took the best of her and she is proper dying and all you see is this hardy face – 'cus he's hiding his fear, its tight on his face – *oh* and its shot in mono-chromatic or whatever it's called **black and white,** dedicated black and white, 'cus this story is going to be like *art,* but not some shitty French thing where you come out the pictures looking for the nearest Oak to hang a noose from and swiiiing, I mean proper art, *art-art,* art that is like <u>art</u>, but is also commercial, Ken Loach meets Adam Sandler that sort of thing, but shot…you know, beautifully…and he – the lead character – he's built.

(Shows built)

And he's got the eyes.

(Shows wide eyes)

Which sort of throws you because he looks like Adonis but he's also got this sensitive thing going on, which you show in the opening scene when he says, right to the camera, like he's talking directly to us, like he's talking specifically to you, but he is really talking to his father, who turns up at the hospital too late *toooo fucking late –*

(Bitter)

– let us be in no doubt about that he is too late. **Because he's a cunt!**

(Emotional/collects himself)

And he is a cunt, the dad character he is a proper cunt. The dad *who should have been there at the end* but was up to his nuts in the mum's best friend – which is why she got the cancer in the first place if you ask me, but that is an aside, a subtext if you like, and we don't know that, the cancer link, the audience don't see that, but we get a sense of it, all that we really know is that she is a bag of bones, and she is yellow in the eyes with death and that her illness is a *cancer of repressed sorrow and pain* that she caught from her being exposed to massive betrayal...she witnesses – this is where she is exposed, and we show this in the early scenes – she witnesses the ultimate betrayal when she arrives home from work – this is what she tells the son character, he wasn't there, he's seventeen, he's at college, only ever kissed a girl, he's a slow starter, so sex and betrayal – *no idea*. She's been at work all day, ten hours, mending broken people, she is fragile the mother, she is a *soul*, and she's treating heroin addicts in the hospital but she is as brittle as a soul – beautiful spiritual energy – she arrives home – this would work great in the middle act, it's based on my own mum and dad *sort of,* but not exactly – although my mum did die of cancer and my dad is a cunt – she arrives home finds him shagging her best mate, in their bed – she kicks off – well you would wouldn't ya – the mum character kicks off, he drags her down the stairs – not difficult, she's seven stone on a fat day and he's a throbbing lump – drags her by her hair, bangs her face and nose and mouth off every sharp object in the house, leaves her buckled and bleeding in the front garden like some crippled dog.

Beat/reflects/is this film or his life?

GARY (CONT'D)
God there's so many layers. I'm probably not pitching it great am I…I'm losing myself…

Looks at the hourglass/time is escaping him.

GARY (CONT'D)

OK. OK. The energy, I can feel the energy coming back. The son character. He finds out about all this – he's a little bit *Edmund* you know, wild, angry, Edmond the bastard, King Lear?

(Breaks into a rendition of King Lear)

Why bastard. Wherefore base when my dimensions are as well compact, my mind as generous, and my shape as true, as honest madam's issue? Why brand us they with base? With baseness? Bastardy? Base, base – he, the son character, he finds out. About the beating. The neighbours call him from college, they've found the mum in a puddle of *thick red* on the hard pavement, they've put her in a taxi, and they've called the son who collects his mum from the hospital *practically in a bucket*. She's walking wounded. Nose all over her face, clumps of hair missing, bald patches where he's ripped the locks clean off her head *beautiful pretty face* a rainbow of colours *a rainbow* – he collects her and takes her home – but she never recovers, you don't do you, not from that kind of abuse, she hardly speaks for months.

(Reflects)

The voice withdraws in shame...then the cancer – that's what happens ain't it, first the abuse, then the shame, fathom deep shame, then the pressing down of the pain, then the cancer – but that's the end of the film, that's the end scene when the audience is like whoaaaaa did not see that coming ffffffff, and even when the police come round – this is in the middle of the third act, after the dad lobs the mum over the stair-railing and calls her a *spunk sucking prostitute* which broke my mum more than the beating he gave her out on the pavement 'cus she only ever had sex with one man her entire life and that was my dad – when the police come round, in the film, she won't open her mouth, she won't say a word, she covers for him, that is how loyal and beautiful she is she covers for the ***twat*** and the police – listen to this you'll think I've made it up, *I wish I had* – the police give her a warning – they give *her* a warning what kind of fucked up policing is that – says it was her own fault and she should keep away from him, the dad.

(Incredulous)

She covered for him.

(Deep breath/gathers himself)

Good scene.

(Beat)

Get the audience, that. Right there.

(Touches his heart)

Sets up the end scene, **I am pure love,** the finale, the pay off.
So the son cares for the mum, even though he is only seventeen –

(Goes Shakespearean again)

– this body, this machine that my soul is in, it is vulnerable, innocent…you betrayed me…you're my father, you're supposed to be there for me, keep me secure, love me, take care of me.

(Long beat)

This is what the son character could probably say. To the dad. He's seventeen, he can't even care for himself, he's the runt, he is only five foot five, but he is quirky, he's odd, he's got a delicious edge. He nurses the mum – and he does talk to the dad, of course he does, he has it out with him one-to-one, he's only a boy still but he tells him straight, *you threw my mum down a flight of stairs. You are not my dad any more. You are my friend.*
But you are not my dad…you left all this shit on my plate.

(Angry)

Look at me I'm still picking up the shit.

(Beat/reflective)

I like doing that. Picking up the shit. I'll tell you why I like doing that! It's payback for the early years. The favours you did me.

(Insistent)

*Not love…*favours.

(Laughs)

The mum character says – this is where the comedy comes in, I don't want to be typecast, I want people to see that I can write action and drama *and* sex – because the son, listen to this, you'll love this little twist *I'll come back to the comedy*, this has got everything this story – we're not even 10 minutes into the film when bang! A graphic sex scene where the boy rents his skinny little teenage bones to dirty old bastards in the public toilets in the town just to earn some money to pay off his dad's debts – a grand to pay off his gambling addiction because the bailiff is kicking his front door in every other day and giving the dad depression. The debt gets paid, the dad gets his reprieve and the boy gets an arse hole like a clown's pocket – and the mum the mum the mum I was telling you about the comedy the mum goes *what favours did he ever do for you?* And the son goes – it's funny he goes, he goes –

(Thinks of an example, struggles)

He did me favours lots of favours. But he can't think of a single one. Not a one. The mum goes – she folds her arms like that.

(Folds his arms)

She goes *come on, what favours did he ever do you?* The son thinks for a few seconds and then... *he gave me a lift to college one day.* And the mum goes *that was once, and only because he had to pass the college to get to the pub.* Funny scene. *Favours, what fucking favours?*

(Laughs)

He used to try and give me mentoring talks, my dad, did I tell you that, mentoring, me! *Life is a bitch son* he said *life is a bitch that's why God gave us drugs and gambling and sex so we could cope with it.*

(Angry)

Life is a bitch, *tell me something I don't know you old bastard. I don't want your shitty mentoring talks – I should be mentoring you.*

(Beat/reflective/sad)

I don't think he was ever a dad. It wasn't that kind of relationship. It was a relationship based on favours. He doesn't tell him all this to his face, he writes to him, he tells it all in a letter. *I forgive you* – this is what the boy says – *I forgive you but you're not my dad any more.*

(Chokes/anger and emotion)

And when you are old. And when you are *properly* old and in an old people's home and you are properly alone and no one wants you any more, I'm going to come to that old people's home and I'm going to pay back those favours. You did me favours *not love* – you gave me lifts to places – and I'm going to pay you back.

(Voice breaks)

The bruises heal, the heart does not.

(Beat)

The mum says that. Good line.

(Beat)

Then the cancer gets her.

(Beat)

She can't find a way to bleed her pain so it's pressed down and turned in. Root-bound.

Cancer. The boy reads up on it, studies every page he can find on cancer, becomes an expert on cancer at seventeen – he doesn't want to be studying cancer, who wants to make their young life a cancer study *he wants to take her place <u>he</u> wants to die!*

He wants to swallow the contents of a chemist shop or swing from the nearest Oak because that would be easier than having to watch his mother...his mother...

(Emotion/Beat)

He should be climbing trees he should be chasing girls he should be studying for exams and dreaming of going to Uni – I *was going to be a film maker, making movies, or acting or something, I hadn't even made my mind up yet, that was my dream,* not googling the most painless way to leave this world by your own hand – his mum *asks* him – and she knows it's a mortal sin to take your own life, people that take their own life end up walking the endless corridors of Dante's Purgatorio relentlessly doing their life review over and over and over until their sin is cleansed...he tells her that. This is in an earlier scene when the agony has diseased her thinking and she's looking for the ultimate pain relief – *please help me to die* – he is clammy with sorrow this boy, clammy wet and spent with the weight of her suffering this runt this small bundle of quirk *please help me to die son* she says and all he keeps thinking all he keeps thinking all he keeps thinking is *please, please, please mum help __me__ to die!*

(Beat)

Cancer is not kind.

(Beat)

Cancer is no respecter of age.

(Beat)

It is not a spectator sport, I know that much.

(Beat)

They said that the cancer would give her two months. That's how they said it, like the cancer was in charge now, the disease was in command now, it wasn't the doctors or the nurses but the cancer that had decided *she had two months left to live.*

(Beat)

The mother finds cancer in her bones. The son finds *suicide web-sites* on the World Wide Web. The father finds religion in the Good Book – *fucking religion* that's fucking convenient *gambling would be safer dad at least it's fucking honest...*

(Beat)

The dad promises that God will save the mum, and that she won't die and he says all this in phone calls and notes on Facebook and texts on the mobile phone because he can't find his way to the hospice. No that's not true, he can find his way to the hospice but he won't, because he knows, *he knows...*if he sees her cancer he sees the truth: it's *his* cancer, the cancer *he* gave her. Not when he had sex with her best friend and not when he threw her down two flights of stone stairs and beat her like a dog in the street. The cancer he gave her when he told my mum that she was a prostitute.

A beat.
Emotion.

He has lost the film somewhere and fallen into his own story.
He recognises this.
He collects himself.

GARY (CONT'D)
So the mum is tangled up in the black-cancer and the dad is distracted by the holy dove and the boy is busy googling death and making juices and trying to get her body alkaline, because the books say that cancer can't live in an alkaline body, and the dad, he's talking in texts and hiding in scriptures and saying *God will save her,* but the son knows that God can't save her, but maybe the dad can, maybe *he* can…but he won't even help with the juices… *don't need juices* he says, *I've done some prayer*s and that's the bit of the film that goes boooooooom *man* it hits you so hard you feel as though you've fallen from a tree, *God can't save her but he can, the father can,* just by turning up, just by showing his face, just by being in the room he wouldn't even have to speak, he wouldn't even need a line, just a walk on part would be enough, *just show your face you twat* but he is a ***fucking coward*** because he won't look at ***his*** cancer he hides from ***his*** cancer in a fucking church hall singing hymns and saying *leave it to God.* ***FUCK GOD!*** *I do not believe in God.*

(Angry/aimed directly at the shadowy figure)

God might be my Father but *you* are not my friend.

(Beat)

This is what the son says and this is what is going to make this a film that people crawl away from, crawl like a creeping thing, like someone has walked into the cinema and thrown a truth-grenade and said *have some of that*!

(Beat)

The dad does not make the hospice and the mum dies at 5.15 in the morning. She dies in the boys arms and he is holding her like she held him when he was a baby, he is holding her and shussing her and comforting her *the dad should have been there* but the dad was not and the son is holding her as she goes, as the body dies, as the spirit bursts out of the coil he *feels* it, he feels it leave and he wants to go with her, he wants to follow.

(Long beat)

And then there's this, this. Confusion.

(He is confused)

Is he holding his dying mother in his arms? Or...is someone holding *him* in their arms? Is it the other

way around? Is he dying? Maybe…maybe the boy
– he *was* distraught, the boy was suffering after she
died in his arms, *so much pain so much sorrow* –
maybe he couldn't bear it any longer and maybe he
did something *unfortunate*…to himself…

(Directly to the shadowy figure)

I didn't really mean to, I promise you that much, I
wasn't thinking straight, I wasn't thinking at all I…

He stops himself.
He realises that he has fallen into first person, he is
talking about himself again, and not the character.
He stands.
He takes a breath
Steady again.

GARY (CONT'D)
I don't think the son character…if he does hang
himself from a tree, I don't think he really means
to do it, he was not in his right mind, his mind had
left him way before he climbed the Oak tree, and
noosed his young neck with old rope and…jumped.
Jumped from the Oak in a fit of despair, he did it
in a moment of **deep** anguish, an insanity…because
– and the audience might not understand this, but
it is important that the they do understand this, I
don't want them to hate the boy he was just lost

in the pain – the rope around his neck is balm. It is comfort, because even breathing *in the world* without his mum is lashes to this poorly boy and sliding out of the coil is like taking off a seventeen year old straight jacket. Balm.

(Long beat)

I can't look at that part yet. I haven't worked that bit out. That's the part I'm still not clear on. I feel as though I can't finish the story.

(Beat)

I can't move on to the next scene until I've concluded the last scene. I know that at the end of the story the boy feels...*heaven*, that's clear, that is the end scene definitely, he sees beings of light all around him, beautiful beings holding him in their arms, cradling him *in their arms*, shussing him, loving him.

(Breaks down/sobs)

And he's saying over and over and over *oh my mum oh my mum oh my beautiful mum* and that is when he realises that there is no such thing as death – he sees it, and that is what the audience get, that's the payoff – *there is no death*. And even better than that – this is where he turns to the camera – he has become a glowing being himself, hovering above the ground and glowing like Swayze in Ghost – this is at the beginning of the film and this is where it ends, the final scene, he looks at the camera – and the audience suddenly get it, **he is dead** – and we're in close on his face, its radiating, bliss and he says…

In the corner of his eye he catches the timer as the last grains of sand fall through the neck of the glass.
Close on the hourglass timer.
His 20 minutes allotted time has elapsed.
His pitch is over.
Gary looks at the shadowy figure behind the table and smiles.

GARY (CONT'D)
I am pure love.

Silence.
Gary looks at the shadowy figure for a response.
There is no response.
He turns.
A last look.
Nothing.
Gary exits the room

CUT TO:

EXT. HOTEL ROOM – DAY

CLOSE ON a door in the hallway of a generic, anonymous hotel-like establishment.
*On the door is a sign: **Purgatorio Films – The 20 Minute Film Pitch.***
Pull back to see:
Gary is sitting outside on a chair, waiting.
He is alone.
His head is slumped.
He is still holding his script.
He did not succeed with his last pitch, clearly.
He looks at the front page for a few seconds.
He looks at the title as though reminding himself why he is here.
*It reads: **Life Review. Gary Smith***
He takes a deep breath.
A commanding voice behind the door calls:

VOICE
Gary Smith.

Gary stands and walks to the closed door.
He takes a deep breath, readies himself.
He reaches for the door handle but hesitates.
He retracts his hand.
He does not open the closed door.
He simply walks through the solid wood like a ghost.

SLAM CUT TO:

The next door along: **Barzakh Films – The 20 Minute Film Pitch.**

SLAM CUT TO:

The next door: **Gehenna Movies – The 20 Minute Film Pitch.**

And the next door: **Cold Sleep Pictures – The 20 Minute Film Pitch.**

We sweep around and see similar rooms for as far as the eye can see in an infinite, endless corridor of rooms.

They disappear into a gossamer of divine light.

Each room a similar sign on the door.

End

www.the20minutefilmpitch.com
www.geoffthompson.com